AUTISM in APRIL

April J. Lisbon, Ed.D.

AUTISM in APRIL

A Mother's Journey During the Tween Years

April J. Lisbon, Ed.D.

Copyright April J. Lisbon, Ed.D.

ISBN: 978-0-9998493-0-9
Running Your Race Publishers

Cover Design: GraphixMotion
Interior: Avventura Press

Contact:
dr.lisbonpeoples@gmail.com

Social Media:
www.facebook.com/theadvocacycoach
https://twitter.com/raiseurvisions
www.linkedin.com/in/aprillisbonpeoples

No parts of this book may be reproduced without permission.

DEDICATION

This book is dedicated to my children
who have kept me on my toes as I try to navigate
this Autism journey.

TABLE OF CONTENTS

DEDICATION 5

TABLE OF CONTENTS 6

INTRODUCTION 7

UNDERSTANDING AUTISM AS A PRACTITIONER 9

THIS AUTISM LIFESTYLE 17

READY, SET, TWEEN YEARS...23

GOOD-BYE FIRST YEAR OF MIDDLE SCHOOL 33

GETTING INTO THE GROOVE OR NOT 39

SOCIAL ACCEPTANCE OR REJECTION.........................49

WHEN THE FLOOD RAGES, WHAT NEXT?...................57

WORDS OF INSPIRATION 65

FINAL THOUGHTS 91

REFERENCES 93

INTRODUCTION

I'm new to this lifestyle called Autism Spectrum Disorder (ASD). One would think that working in the world of special education as a school psychologist for the past 17 years, I would have some idea about any and everything there is to know about ASD, but I don't. Like you, I am trying to better understand what causes ASD, why more children and adults are being diagnosed with ASD, and how I can support an individual with ASD.

My name is Dr. April J. Lisbon and I am the parent of a child with Autism Spectrum Disorder. This journey of understanding ASD as a parent has been quite challenging over the last few years. I am constantly trying to gain some insight as to what behaviors are associated with ASD and those that are developmentally appropriate based on my child's age. Unfortunately, my child only had a few hallmarks that were consistent with Autism Spectrum Disorder. Those unfamiliar with my child assumed that he was a typical child and could not be on the spectrum. Yet looks can be deceiving even for a professional like myself who has been trained to work with individuals with cognitive, behavior, adaptive, and social and emotional delays.

Rather than writing this book solely from the perspective of a school psychologist, I've decided to write this book through the eyes of a mom who's on a journey trying to be the best parent she can be while raising a child with ASD. Specifically, as I share this journey, my goal is to learn about ASD through the eyes of my own child through conversations and daily interactions, wherever this journey will take us.

Initially, this book will briefly discuss my understanding of ASD from the perspective of a school psychologist as well as that of a mom who's raising a child with ASD.

Then as my child shares his feelings with me, the second part of this book will chronicle some of my son's journeys as a tween and some of the fears I have experienced along the way.

The final section of this book will focus on words of encouragement and wisdom that may help you relieve some angst you may feel during these years. You can gain a better understanding of how to help your tween(s) along this awkward phase in life. I also want you to take the time to note your thoughts and emotions as you move through the process of reading this book. I've even provided you with a few places in this book to help you get started, or you can even buy a paper journal.

It is my hope after you've read our story that as a mom, you'll feel empowered to learn more about ASD through your child's eyes and not through what you read or hear from others. It's important that the voices of individuals with ASD be heard so that we, as their advocates, may better prepare them for the highs and lows they will encounter in this world. So today, I make myself available to begin this journey I call *Autism in April*.

UNDERSTANDING AUTISM as a PRACTITIONER

Parenthood is a funny thing. It doesn't come with a manual and each child and his or her needs are different. Not different because of the child, but different in the sense that you, as their parent, may not always know how to handle their actions, attitudes, and behaviors.

You've taken the time to read parenting books. You've taken the time to listen to family, friends, and co-workers share their stories about parenthood but nothing, and I mean NOTHING, prepares you to be a parent of a child with Autism Spectrum Disorder (ASD).

When I first learned about the big A word, Autism, I was taking an undergraduate psychology class. The more I learned about the disorder I became fascinated with how the mind worked and how different the lived experiences of these individuals would be. It seemed like they marched to their own drum beat, some verbal and others nonverbal. I mean with all the research that was being conducted on Autism back then I wanted to know one thing—why couldn't anyone tell me what caused Autism? Honestly, the professor may have shared some ideas back in those days, but it was irrelevant to me as I didn't know anyone with Autism. Yet the question always remained, what is Autism?

Eventually I decided to pursue my career as a school psychologist based on my love for understanding the human mind and how it functions. The idea of working with children had always been my focus and school psychology filled my professional needs back then. In my graduate program, we learned about various disabilities including Autism Spectrum Disorder and its implications in the school setting. The more I learned about ASD and other disability classifications, the more I wanted to work with younger children. I was a strong supporter of early intervention and felt like being a preschool school psychologist was my life's calling. I vowed in my heart that I would advocate for those who could not advocate for themselves.

After completing graduate school, I was assigned three school settings and was also assigned as one of three school psychologist who solely focused on preschoolers. It was my first job and I thought I knew any and everything there was to know about special education and how to educationally diagnosis children, especially young children, with disabilities. Umm...not so much. I soon discovered that I had a lot to learn about special education and identifying children with disabilities as not every child was the classic textbook case I was taught while in graduate school.

Yes, that one size fits all mentality does not work well in the realm of school psychology as there are so many factors (e.g. environmental, cultural, etc.) that makes it challenging to determine if a disability exists. I learned a lot as a newbie in the field and had a great support system during my early years, which helped me rethink how I assessed children as well as how we as teams would identify these children. Labeling children has lasting effects not only on the psyche of children but also their parent(s) so I'm cognizant of how I work with my students, teachers, and families before, during, and after my role ends during the special education process.

I need to share this information with you before we move any further in this book as even prior to having children with special needs, the idea of incorrectly labeling a child with a disability scared me. What if the reason for referral was incorrect? What if I'm testing environmental stressors (e.g. trauma in the home or community)? There had been so many personal what-ifs throughout my career that even I was initially leery about having my own children receive early intervention services let alone school-based service. I eventually had to learn professionally and personally that I needed to get beyond the what-ifs and do what was in the best interest of children including my own.

Now, as I sit here in my room typing with only the light of a Himalayan glow lamp while everyone is asleep, I realized that I have so many cases that I can think about that have transformed my life professionally and personally. The ones that changed me the most where those cases of ASD as every child was different and only a handful aligned with the common characteristics of ASD that I learned about during my graduate school training. For the purposes of this book, I'll share with you two of my trickiest cases that gave me a newfound respect for individuals who have diagnoses of ASD. My educational level nor my professional experiences prepared me on how to handle these cases.

I am reminded of one of my first cases that occurred either during my second or third year as a school psychologist, where I'd worked with a preschooler who seemed to be a typically developing child who presented more with language delays that impacted his cognitive skills. I mean when I interviewed the parents, the child always had some form of language and never lost this language. This child enjoyed being touched and engaged in nonverbal social exchanges. The only concern of the parents and the school team at that time for this young preschooler was language. It may have been hard for others to understand him (he did exhibit some echolalic behaviors) BUT it was not in the same manner that is often associated with individuals with ASD. According to Grossi, Marcone, Cinquegrana, and Gallucci (2013), "Echolalia is a language disorder, commonly defined as 'a meaningless repetition in echo of speech'" (p. 904). However, as these authors pointed out, echolalia is also associated with other neurological (e.g. aphasia) and psychiatric (e.g. schizophrenia) disorders. Without going into a lengthy discussion, aphasia disorders impact a person's ability to use language to communicate.

The idea of this child having ASD was far from any of our minds as the referral and the behaviors of the child at that time did not point to ASD and when I worked with the child individually and observed him at his preschool center, he presented as a typical child who had trouble with language. The team agreed that this child required special education services to meet his needs. The team, including parents, agreed that the child's language had a large impact on his global development. Therefore, at the initial meeting, the child was found eligible to receive services as a student with developmental delays and speech and language services would be provided as a related service. Case closed.

Not so fast, mommies. Not so fast.

Why, you might ask? Well, after a year of services, the child began exhibiting some behaviors that were not exhibited or even described by parents or his previous teacher when the team first met. The child's language regressed and he began exhibiting behaviors that were not seen previously (e.g. climbing on book shelves, hitting peers, head banging). When the email came from my team members at the time, I was in complete shock as this was not the child I'd worked with the previous school year. Everyone agreed that we needed to reconvene to discuss this child's case a little deeper as something was missing and we needed to place our finger on it so that we could do what was in the best interest of the child.

As a team, we clearly knew that this child required special education services to help him be successful both at home and at school. We also knew that it was not uncommon for young children to display different attitudes, actions, and behaviors as the truth is, depending on the situation, we all may exhibit changes in our attitudes, actions, and behaviors depending on the situation. It's human nature. However, as a new professional in the field, I'd never expected that within a year timeframe that our team would be back together discussing the possibility of Autism Spectrum Disorder for this child. At that moment in time in my career, I literally questioned if I knew what I was doing as a school psychologist as how could I have missed the classic symptoms often associated within individuals with ASD based on my educational training. As a practitioner I felt horrible because I knew that if I'd recognized it the first time the child's individualized education plan (IEP) may have been written differently. Or maybe this is hindsight since I have more experience as a practitioner now and have my own child with ASD. Either way I felt bad that I had not recognized the possibility of ASD the first time around.

Rather than taking this case on solo, I worked hand in hand with one of our veteran preschool school psychologist who had formal training in working with individuals with Autism Spectrum Disorder. She reassured me that based on the information in my report I had made the right call the first time and that not all children who may have characteristics of Autism Spectrum Disorder would easily fit on a check off list as I'd learned in graduate school. I breathed a sigh of relief as I watched her working with the same child I had worked with before.

That session was an eye opener for me as I had no clue who this new child was. He still had some language concerns, but it seemed like his behaviors had regressed. The child was more aggressive and easily agitated. Not at all like the child I had worked with before.

After all assessments were completed, our team reconvened to re-determine if this child's eligibility classification would change. Indeed, it had, and the child met our school district's criteria for Autism. Even as the results were being read I asked myself what I had initially done wrong. I truly felt like it was my fault that this child had been misdiagnosed the first time around. When my veteran school psychologist saw my face at the meeting, she continued to reassure me as she'd done in the past that I made the correct call the first time. She shared with me that Autism is a tricky diagnosis because it looks different in every child. There are always markers (e.g. stemming) that most, if not all children with ASD will exhibit. Some are subtler then others. Yet all we can do as school psychologists is to address the child in the here and now and not be anxious about what we believe may happen in the future.

She was right! It was then as a practitioner that I stopped beating myself up about this case and those that I would have in the future as I realized that my role was to answer the referral question presented by the team and to use measures that would address it.

Now don't get me wrong, over time I have conducted more assessments even if they were not a part of the referral based on information that may have been shared by the parent(s) or in my working with the child. More times than not, my gut instincts and experience would kick in and the result may not have been what the team originally suspected. This was the case in the second example I will share.

For this second case I'm presenting to you, I will tell you that I was a more seasoned school psychologist when I first approached this case. I was starting my 12th year in the field and working in my first urban school district. This case wasn't like the others. The individual who was being initially referred for special education was a middle schooler—an 8th grader. I vividly remember this case as many individuals presumed that this teen presented with an emotional disturbance. The child was extremely aggressive, had a short fuse, and had been suspended from multiple schools. But something just didn't sit well with me on this case. There seemed to be more going on than a child with oppositional or conduct-like behaviors.

I know this isn't politically correct, but I remember "stalking" this child in school. I would conduct observations in the classroom and out of the classroom. I would even invite this child to check in with me in the mornings or whenever needed to ensure that he was having a good day. The more I learned about him, the more I realized that his behavior patterns were not that of a typical teenager. Dare I say that my gut told me that this child had similar character traits of individuals identified with ASD.

When I presented my thoughts to school personnel and the family prior to signing consent for the evaluation, several individuals at the table were shocked by this idea, because the focus for many years had been the behaviors. Yet when I presented my observational findings and my conversations with the child, everyone agreed that we should assess for Autism as well. I'm so thankful that we were all on the same page as a great weight had been lifted off the family's shoulders. Indeed, this student had characteristics of individuals with ASD based on multiple sources. As a sidebar, this teenager became my school-based son as it seemed like every time my biological son had issues in school, so did he, and vice versa. I always knew what the day would be like based on whether a discipline referral was made for my school-based son.

Let me not bore you with my stories as a professional in the field of school psychology as this book is not about me. Besides I have too many stories like these that I can share with you, but I do not want to distract you away from the purpose of this book. Nevertheless these two cases changed my practice as a school psychologist and eventually a parent of a child with ASD.

THIS AUTISM *LIFESTYLE*

Where is the manual on parenting children? I can recall many times when my mother would tell me that I should enjoy being a child for as long as possible because being an adult is hard. How could this be? I mean adults drove cars, made TONS of money, and always seemed to have more fun than kids.

Well I sadly learned that there is a difference between how a child and an adult views life. Adulting is not what it's cracked up to be as it's extremely challenging balancing one's personal and professional lifestyles. Add one or more children to the mix and it's not only one person you are caring for but multiple people. Little people who depend on you for their basic human needs can at times be scary especially when you are a first-time parent. I'll ask again, where is the parenting manual? Since there isn't one, I simply share with you my parenting journey of gaining a better understanding on what ASD is and raising a child with ASD.

Autism Spectrum Disorder is a developmental syndrome that is neurologically based. It impacts individuals' ability to engage in social reciprocity and communicate their needs, and they may engage in restricted and repetitive behaviors (American Psychiatric Association, 2000). Boys are diagnosed more often than girls with ASD. According to Lord and Bishop (2010), the greatest risk factor for being ASD is male; Autism occurs about four times more often in boys than girls. Blumberg et al. (2013) reviewed information from the Center for Disease Control (CDC) Autism and Developmental Disabilities Monitoring (ADDM) and found that from 2002–2008 the rise of ASD diagnoses increased by 78%. Most referrals for ASD were made by parents of school age children according to their research. With the rise of ASD diagnoses over the years, some families may find it to be an uphill battle finding support for their child.

Parenting a child with Autism Spectrum Disorder can be tricky and outright stressful at times. There are times when I've felt like I really had a grasp on what made my child tick and then there were other times I wondered which child was living in my home. As I write this book, I realize that I am not the only person that feels this way as there is some research to support that families of children with ASD have fewer community resources than families of children with other exceptional needs.

For those families raising a child or children with ASD, Kogan et al. (as cited in Lord & Bishop, 2010) suggested that "... children with ASD are underserved, with more delayed or foregoing healthcare, less family centered-care, and more difficulties with referrals" (p. 3). In an essence, families of children with ASD have more financial struggles and/or may reduce or stop working more often than other groups of families raising children with special needs due to these lack of community resources. Such ongoing stressors may make it difficult for parents to understand the ongoing needs of their child with ASD as they grow older.

Parenting may be stressful in families. Parenting stress can be defined as the level of discomfort or distress an individual may experience in relation to the demands associated with parenting (Hayes & Watson, 2013). Combine this with the lack of community supports and services for a child with ASD and it's a potential recipe for disaster. Then again, this may have only been my personal experiences throughout the years.

Has this been your experience or that of someone else you know? If so, then just know that you're not alone and it's a systemic issue.

As a parent of a child with ASD, have you been trying to figure out or gain a better understanding of what triggers create your child's sensory meltdowns? Guess what? So have I! The truth is individuals with ASD present with various behavioral characteristics that can be mild or severe. It may also be challenging to pinpoint what thing(s) are magnetic triggers that cause sensory discomfort for one's child, which in turn can make it tricky to find that right community based provider(s) to meet the unique needs of YOUR child.

As a parent of a child with ASD there are days when I'm unsure which child I might encounter when I walk through the door. For me, parenting my child with ASD has been an adventure to say the least and it may be why it took me some time to find the right support system for my son throughout the years.

Let me take it a step back and briefly look at some of these behaviors throughout the years.

Reflecting on my child's younger years, he was a typically developing boy who enjoyed life. He loved hugs and kisses. He loved being a daredevil and climbing over tables and furniture. Scared me half to death sometimes but I guess that's what little boys do, right? The only issues that seem to plague my oldest son was that he spoke gibberish (I referred to it as Martian language) and he was a picky eater. I mean a real picky eater.

As a school psychologist I found that it was not uncommon for young children to have preferred foods. Even we as adults may not try new things as it may not be appealing to the eyes or the nose. So, his eating habits weren't a big issue for me at all. I mean throughout my pregnancy I ate strange things (e.g. ramen noodles with beef stir fry which included mangos) and I assumed that my strange food cravings rubbed off on him. No big deal, I said! Until I realized that I needed to buy stock in oatmeal. That's right three meals, seven days weekly my son would only tolerate oatmeal. His favorite snacks were chocolate pudding and Cheetos. Try feeding him anything else and he would scream repeatedly. I eventually stopped trying to give him any new foods as I hated seeing my baby in so much pain. Pain because he couldn't use his words to tell me why he didn't want to try anything else. Was it the smell? Did it look funny? All I heard were these gut-wrenching screams which at times drove me bonkers.

He was still my sweet little boy who simply had this language problem or, so I thought. Around age 2½ I had my son evaluated for in-home services as I knew that his language skills lagged other children his age. My son never lost language and used single words that he would produce clearly. It just seemed like when he tried combining two or more words together it would become jumbled. I'll never forget when the examiner asked me if I thought my child may have Autism. Respectfully, I told him I had not but in my mind, I said if anyone should know the hallmarks of Autism it would be me, the school psychologist!

Blah, blah, blah, blah, blah. This is what I am saying now as today I realized that it is easier to identify developmental challenges in other people's children than your own because of the emotional attachment. My heart would not allow me to believe that my child had ASD because I knew, at that time, how individuals viewed Autism Spectrum Disorder. Sadly, it wasn't nice. I just didn't want my child to experience the teasing, bullying, and/or taunting that often comes with being different. I know this tends to be a lot of parents' fears as children grow older. However, the thought of this happening to my child because of a developmental challenge that was out of his control, really put me on edge.

Without taking you on a long, exhausting, play-by-play of some of my personal fears, I'll simply say that no matter what age or the location, children with Autism Spectrum Disorder will experience some form of teasing and/or bullying by their peers. I know that other children are teased and/or bullied by other children. However, when you witness your child with ASD being teased by same age peers and YOUR child is clueless that he is being teased, it's a hard pill to swallow.

I remember this day like it was yesterday as THIS was the first time that I could no longer deny that I was truly raising a child with ASD. My two boys were participating in a summer camp within our local area and the children were seated in the dugout awaiting their turns to practice their batting swings. Most of the children were using cups to drink water out of the cooler. However, there was one child who wanted to be different—he wanted to drink directly from the spout. My oldest son saw this and told the other child he was nasty for drinking out of the spout. As a mom who dislikes germs, I agreed in my head.

The two boys went back and forth arguing as to whether the other child drank from the spout. This drew a small crowd of other children listening on, awaiting to see who would win the debate. Immediately the other child exclaimed, "That's why you have buck teeth!" to which my child then retorted, "Oh, do you know what my brother calls me?" I had no choice but to chime in and tell my son to move in closer to me for two reasons. First, I realized that my son was oblivious to the fact that he had just been teased about his appearance. Second, because I knew what his younger brother would call him, I knew that the kids would have made fun of him and his feelings would have been hurt. Was I right or wrong for jumping in? I don't know but I personally didn't want to see my child hurt as this was the first time that he wanted to engage in building relationships with other people that weren't at his school.

Not much has changed since that event. It seems like the teasing and bullying has grown over the years and my child is still a target of being bullied. The only difference is that he has learned to tease others, which has led to both verbal and physical altercations with others. In turn this has affected his ability to secure solid relationships with peers his age (he prefers students two grade levels ahead of him), his overall academic progress, and his self-esteem for a couple of years.

Simply put parenting is hard work. It's even more challenging parenting a child with ASD as every day is different. I can't tell you the number of emotional meltdowns I have endured on this journey and days where I've wanted to throw in the towel. There have been times when I've felt like I've failed all my children as I've spent more time trying to control and reduce the number of aggressive outbursts my youngest son has had both at home and school. Being a parent of a child with ASD is exhausting, and at times has drained what little sanity I have.

As an only child, I never had to deal with sibling rivalry, but I know that sibling rivalry is quite normal. However, there are times I feel bad for my youngest son as the teasing and taunting from my oldest child is brutal. No matter how many times I tell my youngest son to stand up to his brother he refuses to do it, as like most siblings, he admires his big brother. He simply cries and will allow his brother to make fun of him until I step in. I have no clue how to make things better as the words *stop it* and *leave him alone* are no longer effective. On a side note, my oldest doesn't mess with his little sister as she is feisty and will tell it like it is. I also think that the age difference makes both boys protectors of her and they allow her to get away with EVERYTHING.

READY, SET, TWEEN YEARS

The tween years. Oh, the tween years. As parents, we are aware that our children have their own personalities and opinions that may not align with our own. I get it. I thought the so called terrible two stage was challenging but these tween years seem to be a nightmare to say the least.

I assumed that the last year of elementary school would have been the easiest as my son was familiar with all his teachers and had made friendships over the last two years. *Piece of cake*, I told myself.

Yet his fifth-grade year seem to be the start of some strange twists and turns that led to a lot of time outs, arguing, and even taking away his prized possessions—technology. I had no choice as my son's grades were decreasing and his behaviors were increasing. Who was this child? This was not the happy go lucky child who was well-mannered and pleasant to be around. This was a new child, one I'd never encountered in my home or at work. I'm assuming some of you are nodding your heads at this very moment in agreement that your child is much different at home than when s/he is with others.

At the start of his fifth-grade year, my son seemed to be really motivated to excel in school. He was doing his homework and was excited about learning. His level of aggression and arguing had decreased from that summer. I knew this would be a great school year as he wanted it to be a great year for himself.

I am unsure if something shifted at school or if it were hormones or the combination of both, but it seemed like my son's behaviors and attitudes towards school changed after the first quarter interim grades came out. His hygiene declined, and he appeared to be moodier than normal. My son refused to speak about school and was only interested in playing with his Legos. He had shut himself off from the world and with his difficulties related to oral expression, he struggled to tell me what was happening to him. I was clueless on how to help my child as I assumed it was just a by-product of the tween years and we simply had to roll with the punches, so to speak.

Then the phone calls started. He had become more physically and verbally aggressive towards individuals at school and at home. During this time, I was commuting anywhere between three and four hours to the city for work. There was no way that I could get home or to school in time enough to help de-escalate his behaviors. My heart sank repeatedly the more the calls and texts came as I had no clue who this child was that was living in my home.

My son's behaviors had become problematic at school to the point that he received multiple in school and out of school suspensions. He had a behavior intervention plan in place per his individualized education plan (IEP) and we reviewed it quite frequently. Yet we, including myself, were clueless on what was happening with him. No matter the case, I was just ready for the school year to end as I didn't want my child's behaviors to impact him to the point that he would be retained in fifth grade. I knew if this occurred his self-esteem would be crushed, and his behaviors would only escalate.

In the end, his grades improved as he was switched to another classroom towards the latter part of the third nine-week period. The new move was the best decision for him at that time as it met his academic, social, and emotional needs. My son was happier, and his actions, attitudes, and behaviors improved at school and home. I was so ecstatic at that time as my son had improved his grades just enough so that he was promoted to sixth grade.

He was excited and so was I as we survived the last year

of elementary school. One hurdle down and a new one to go. I prayed that the change to middle school would be a little easier now that he was going to a school adjacent to the local high school. Yes, you read that correctly, his excitement about being a middle schooler had less to do with being in middle school and more related to the idea that he would be in "high school." I just love how the mind of Autism works and no matter how much I shared that he was not a real high schooler, it didn't matter to him. All he knew was that his middle school shared the same building as the high school.

We had a very relaxing and enjoyable summer vacation that year. We traveled out of state and my son and his siblings were able to connect with family and friends. It was what he, I mean, we ALL needed to escape the highs and lows associated with fifth grade.

As you know, all good things come to an end. It was time for us to return home but the questions came nonetheless. My son wanted to know who his teachers would be. He asked about what he should do if he was unable to remember his locker combination. School hadn't started, and the anxiety was on 100%. I had no clue what to tell him as I hadn't been in a middle school as a student in over 30 years. I reassured him that sixth grade would be a fresh start as he would make new friends and those behaviors and suspensions that held a cloud over his head wouldn't count against him as this was his new beginning. He seemed to accept my train of thinking at that moment.

Sixth grade year started off well. My son was excited about going to school and meeting his teachers. He was interested in finding out how many of his former fifth grade classmates would be in his classes and of course, he was excited about sharing the high school cafeteria as a middle schooler. Things were looking up for him and I was extremely relieved that he felt comfortable at his new school.

The first half of the first nine-week period went off great. Grades were average and there were no calls from administration. I was beyond elated as like some parents, I had grown mentally exhausted with receiving calls of what my son had been doing wrong and less of what he was doing right.

Then a shift happened.

I am unsure what changed after the first interim reporting of that school year, but my son's interest level in school was on the slow decline. He was no longer talking about school and he wasn't turning in assignments. Since I had access to his grades, we would conduct bi-weekly reviews so that he had the ability to ask his teachers for his assignments to improve his grades. His response was "I'll do it because YOU want me to do it" but he wasn't doing it for himself and I had no clue why.

Book checks, binder clean outs, multiple emails, and STILL nothing from my son. It seemed like he couldn't care less about his performance in school. I'd assumed this is a middle school thing because I'd seen it in the past when I worked at the middle school level. Yet, he was my child and I felt like he needed to take school more seriously.

Over time old behaviors started to resurface. He was becoming more argumentative at home and at school. He refused to follow teacher directions. There were some occasions where he became physically aggressive towards peers. In time, the calls began, and I felt like I was living in the Twilight Zone.

At that point, I decided that I would reinvestigate the idea of counseling. Unfortunately, in the area where we resided, individuals were either not accepting new patients or they did not specialize in working with children with ASD. The few we'd tried just weren't a good match for him. I'd gone around and around with this issue the spring of his fifth-grade year and felt defeated. I knew that my son needed help but there wasn't anyone in our area that could help him. I felt emotionally and mentally paralyzed. I would often ask myself if he didn't get his behaviors under control would this be the year that he would either be recommended for a specialized program or possibly expelled from school? I cried so much during that school year, as I was lost.

Has this EVER happened to you? Have you ever searched high and low to find community resources to help you with your child only to be turned away? The frustration was real for me as I felt like I was reliving my son's preschool years all over again. There was a problem but there wasn't a solution. It felt like rejection all over again.

I eventually stopped looking and tried to help him on my own using the techniques I'd used over the years while working with children with exceptional needs as a school psychologist. Let me just say that mommy and school psychologist don't mix as I wasn't hearing him, and he wasn't hearing me. We were at a gridlock more times than not and the "interventions" I tried to implement created an unproductive relationship. We stopped.

I decided that if we couldn't find a therapist in the area to assist with his social and emotional needs, we'd work on the sensory needs. I'm laughing out loud at this moment as trying to find an occupational therapist in our local area at the time was like trying to find a needle in a haystack. Either the numbers were wrong, the individuals were no longer practicing in our area, or they no longer accepted my insurance. Every day I felt like I was failing to take care of my son's needs because every time I turned around, another door was slammed in my face.

We eventually did the best we could as the sixth-grade year progressed. You noticed I didn't refer to this sentence as *his* sixth-grade year as I felt like we were going through this process together.

Winter break finally rolled around, and it was a much-needed break. During that phase in my life, I was getting tired of commuting into the city. I was getting tired of work and feeling like I wasn't making a difference in the students and families I served. I was getting tired of feeling like I was cheating my children out of having a mother who was available to them. I was just downright tired. I needed this vacation to recoup and regroup as I really feared that year I would have a nervous breakdown.

It was the best vacation ever as I didn't think about work and it was a time to just be mom. Yes, I fussed at them when they didn't listen. But I gave more hugs and kisses to let them know that I cared and loved them with all my heart. I even noticed my son's stemming decreased as he was in an environment that was less stressful for him and of course, there wasn't any school work for him to fret over. I needed this. We needed this. We needed us to simply be us.

Upon returning from our vacation, I promised in my heart that I would try one more time to find a therapist in our local area who not only had experience working with tweens but one who specifically had experience working with children with ASD. God, the divine, or the universe or whatever you call YOUR higher power heard me and saw my tears as I received the call. I'd previously left a voicemail message on a potential therapist's phone hoping that there would be availability. The therapist indicated that there were some slots available and encouraged us to schedule an introductory session. I said yes as I had nothing to lose. I'd only hope that my son would respond to this therapist and this would be a good fit for him.

He responded very well to his therapist. My son shared that at his introductory session she was very nice and allowed him to draw and build Legos. *Bingo* I thought to myself. This person heard my son; she recognized that if she wanted him to express his thoughts and emotions it had to come through mediums that he enjoyed and that created the least amount of angst for him. I felt like she really wanted to help us, but I knew the final decision as to whether he wanted to continue working with her was my son's. When he said yes, I'd realized that we were on the right path to helping him feel whole during his tween years. This is not to say that we wouldn't have highs and lows at school and at home. However, to have an unbiased person in his corner was what he needed, we needed, to better support my child with ASD. I'd even signed the release of records form as I knew it would be important for his case manager at that time to connect with his therapist to not only express concerns she may have had regarding my son's behaviors but to also share the positive choices he made at school.

My son always looked forward to therapy and I noticed the calls from school subsiding. The disorganization and low performing grades were still there but he seemed to be much happier since he started therapy. There seemed to be a calm over our home for several weeks until the drama started again.

Let me clear this up as this is something that continues to irk me as a parent of a child with exceptional needs and a school psychologist.

Dear teacher or teachers READ THE IEP!

A lot of the drama that occurred towards the latter part of my son's sixth grade year might have been avoided if teachers simply took the time to first read the present levels of performance pages and the accommodations. As a school psychologist and parent, I am not expecting that you will read all the goals and objectives as those sections are to be closely monitored by the case manager. However, rather than complaining about what kids aren't doing or how their behaviors impact you as an adult, READ THE IEP as the information you seek is already written in black and white.

Even as I write this section I'm finding myself becoming angered once again as a lot of the in-school suspensions and phone calls might have been avoided if individuals read the IEP or teachers and case managers consulted with each other on a frequent basis to see if the actions, attitudes, and behaviors of the child were historical or something new. As a parent, if the actions, attitudes, and behaviors my child is displaying are new I want to know so that we can work on them through therapy. Waiting until a small spark turns into a fire doesn't help you as the teacher or my child.

It had gotten to the point where I questioned as a school psychologist (not mom) as to whether his school was fit to meet his needs. I decided to assemble the school-based team and district personnel. Something needed to be done as my next step was to file a due process complaint against the district. I felt like I had given the school the necessary components, including comprehensive independent psychological and independent neuropsychological reports, to help them better understand the needs of my child. Silence.

As a collective team, we agreed that a private placement or a specialized program was not in the best interest of my son as his grades were too high and when compared to the children at those schools, his behaviors weren't severe enough for him to be reassigned there. I chose to accept the district's position at that time as I was concerned about my son's emotional well-being and having worked in schools that have self-contained classes for children with emotional and behavior disorders, I knew my son was at risk of becoming even more aggressive in such a placement.

In exchange, I requested that the school team enlist the support of the Autism specialist so that the school had a better understanding as to how my child's Autism impacts him personally as well as how it impacts his responses to peers and/or adults within his learning environment. As a school psychologist, I was concerned that this had not been done prior to this meeting in the spring especially since the behaviors were escalating to the point where it felt like the administration was calling me every other day throughout the school year. As a parent, I then began to understand why so many parents file due process complaints against school districts. You send your child to school to learn and if the school is unable to help your child then maybe another school would be more appropriate than his/her home school.

    When the team reconvened, lo and behold the Autism specialist confirmed everything that had been written in my child's comprehensive psychological and neuropsychological. Oh, and did I mention that she also confirmed what was written in his current level of performance during his fifth-grade year? As a team, we agreed to disagree as the goal was for my son to finish out the school year strong. As a parent who's also a school psychologist, I felt like my son's academic needs were being neglected because some individuals failed to understand the true nature of ASD and that one size fits all mentality doesn't work for any child, especially one with ASD. Even I as a school psychologist have had to put myself in check and remind myself that just because I've worked with students with ASD over the years and had great success doesn't mean that I could use those same strategies with my own son. Why? Aside from ASD, all children have their own personalities and temperaments and their response patterns would be different. The same is true for teachers and administrators. Just because you've worked in education for umpteen years or possibly have a special education background doesn't mean that what you've used in the past will work for kids today.

April J. Lisbon

I kept saying two things to myself after that follow up-meeting with school personnel and the district representative. First, even through fear and angst, I vowed in my heart that I would take the pay cut to be closer to my children as they needed me. Second, we would continue therapy as it was the only thing that was going to keep my son afloat for the remainder of his sixth-grade year.

GOOD-BYE FIRST YEAR OF MIDDLE SCHOOL

All I can say is WOW, sixth grade was tough. I know it's not politically correct, but can I say I have a strong dislike for middle school.

The transition from elementary school to middle school is challenging for many children as more times than not, they have been with the same teachers, administrators, and students since kindergarten. Relationships are established. Routines are established. One's identity is established. Once you're in sixth grade, you no longer have your elementary school identity as you're older now. Some of your former elementary school friends may speak to you but sometimes they won't as they've already established new peer relationships the previous school year. I found my son's sixth grade year to be an emotional roller coaster that seemed to never end. I can tell you that there is a marked difference being an educator working in middle school for many years and being the parent of a middle schooler.

I remember when veteran teachers would tell me that once children leave elementary school things were significantly different. I would simply brush these comments off as I would always tell myself that it should be different because the children are getting older and becoming mature. Yet nothing, and I mean nothing, prepared me for sixth grade.

As they told me on numerous occasions, the job of teachers in elementary school is to nurture students to be good learners and citizens. In middle school, the land of the in-between, teachers no longer nurture students to be good learners and citizens. Instead, their roles are to allow them to learn to fly on their own (with some supervision) before high school. I too witnessed this as a school psychologist having been assigned to various grade levels, including middle school. Yet during those years, it never impacted me as it was always someone else's child and not my own.

Unfortunately, my son's first year of middle school significantly impacted him emotionally and mentally. We had highs and a lot of lows including academic and behavior challenges intermittently throughout that year. My son's academic progress was like a roller coaster, filled with unexpected twists and turns that had me screaming and breathing a sigh of relief all at the same time. We butted heads so much that school year. As I shared previously, he displayed such a nonchalant attitude towards school that I ended up taking away his technology and other toys so that he could focus more. As I've always taught my children, education comes first and playing is secondary as the same effort you put into playing (i.e. technology) is the same effort you can put into your education. Besides one day the very education they acquire at school could help them develop a more advance form of technology or toy that they could patent, and people would buy their products. This seemed to fall on deaf ears most times but one day it will sink in.

My son with ASD and I are two strong-willed individuals. We both wore each other down that school year to the point where we would see who would cave in and say forget it. Let the chips fall where they may seemed to be our mantra.

Neither one of us caved as we are cut from the same cloth, I guess. By the end of the school year, he was able to improve his grades enough to move on to the next grade. We survived that school year, barely, but we survived it.

After that school year, I couldn't wait for summer vacation to start as I was mentally and emotionally done with work and school for my children. We all needed a break and to learn how to spend quality time with each other. Change was on the horizon and a vacation was a must for us. Otherwise we would have exploded emotionally as it simply was too much the last school year.

Once it was all said and done, it was time to travel south. We had a lot of people to see and not enough time to get everything done. Spending quality time and building trusting and lasting relationships had been missing from my son in sixth grade and he needed this break to recuperate before starting seventh grade.

As the school year slowly came to a close and summer break was upon us, my anxiety levels were high. Why? I knew that before our summer vacation was over my son would be worried about the upcoming school year. It's like clockwork. Counting down the days and asking when we would leave was inevitable even if it were only the third or fourth day of our vacation. From a few years of experience, I realized that once again I had to prepare my son for the transition back to school. I knew there would be some angst as to whether his teachers from sixth grade would still remember him. In my mind I kept saying, *Who could ever forget your warm smile and good manners?* Yet I realized his concerns were more related to whether they would remember his verbal and physical outbursts towards peers and/or adults. I did my best to calm his fears and reminded him that each school year was a fresh start and a new beginning. Until the new school year begun, we would have an enjoyable vacation.

This year like every year we headed further south to visit family and friends. I would find myself once again out of state at some type of professional event. I was a little worried about leaving him with others as the summer prior he was verbally aggressive towards other family members. I could only hope and pray that this year would be different and that he'd learn to identify his feelings before his feelings overtook him.

The results were in.

My oldest son did great. He was responsive to redirection and was less verbally aggressive towards his siblings and other adults. Even his stemming behaviors had reduced significantly while I was away. All I could think about was what a difference one year made in his life.

The difference? He met with his therapist prior to our leaving for vacation. His therapist provided him with some structural techniques to help reduce his anxiety and his need to lash out at others. I felt like our family was finally in a good place.

I did say that we were in a good place, right? Well if you know anything about Autism Spectrum Disorder you know that these "good places" are sometimes short-lived.

It seemed like as the time drew closer to us returning home from vacation his behaviors began to escalate. He was moodier than normal and snapped at his younger brother a lot, often unprovoked. I also began noticing that his stemming activities increased. Not his traditional hyper- focused jumping but a lot of head twisting and humming while seated. Normally he is aware of his stemming and will tell you that he's exercising. This time around he seemed oblivious to it like there was something on his mind.

So being the psychologist that I am, I asked him if anything was bothering him. As any parent or adult who's been around pre-teens or teens, the answer is often *nothing*. The more I probed, the more agitated he seem until I left it alone. I know he enjoys being on vacation as well as returning home. However, there's a part of me that wonders if he was ready to return home. We returned home from vacation and he was excited about things to come. Both he and his brother were starting martial arts and he was simply ready to return to his own room, toys, and bed. The aggressive behaviors that were noticeable towards the end of our vacation were not seen for several days. But still the school psychologist in me knew that this was the calm before the storm.

I wasn't right or wrong in my thought processes about my son. After returning to therapy after an almost two months hiatus, the truth came out. My son was overly anxious about starting seventh grade this year as nothing would be the same from his vantage point. His case manager who supported him with graciousness and his favorite administrator (i.e. his bowtie buddy) were assigned to different schools.

As his mother, I too shared in his level of anxiety at the end of his sixth-grade year as I wondered if the replacements would be able to handle his behaviors when they occurred. In layman's terms, I wondered if I would be receiving more than the normal number of calls this school year because of his behaviors. So yes, I am on pins and needles awaiting what will occur throughout the new school year. I'm hoping for the best as he's already had one full year in middle school. Only time will tell how this will all unfold.

I'll stop talking your ear off as once again this book is not about me but about gaining an even deeper understanding of the highs and lows often associated with Autism Spectrum Disorder. With you as the reader, we will be walking this journey together as I have no idea what will happen throughout this writing process. What I do know is that the more we learn about ASD from individuals with ASD the better chance we'll have in helping them lead a successful life.

Are you ready? Let's begin. It's time to unpack Autism Spectrum Disorder (ASD) through the eyes of one child, my child.

GETTING INTO THE GROOVE OR NOT

Summer had begun to wind down and thoughts of starting a new school year were upon us. Everyone seemed very excited about the new year although my oldest was anxious about what the new school year would bring. Like any normal teen, he wanted to know his schedule and when business night would be. Yet his body language and verbal language were becoming less and less congruent.

For the last five years, I've always started the new school year three weeks prior to my children as I worked in another locality out of our state. So, I'd never known how anxious my child had been from year to year since when I arrived home, his behaviors were more that of a child who missed a parent that had been gone for a long period of time. He would ask for his normal hugs—more like extended squeezes in his case for sensory input but for us, this was normal.

This school year the changes started off rather slowly and seemed to increase in frequency. He went from mild localized stemming to more extreme stemming which also included more than average vocalization. As every week passed my son would begin jumping and flapping his arms uncontrollably in his preferred locations, his bedroom and the bathroom. He went from brief 3-5 minutes stemming to a full 10 minutes the closer we approached the new school year. There were times I noticed more scripted language that I thought had ended at the end of second grade. Language I hadn't heard or seen during the summer months or during the regular school year were more pronounced now more than ever.

Had these behaviors been hidden from me all these years?

Honestly, I don't know but I had to get to the bottom

of this before the new school year started since I didn't want my son's anxious behaviors to consume him so much that it would make his seventh-grade year unbearable.

How was I going to do this? Initially I thought about sitting him down and asking him what was going on in his mind. However, knowing my son, he would tell me nothing was going on or he was simply exercising the wiggles out. I even thought about taking him to get a massage but for now it was out of the budget. Besides, I'm unsure if there are massages geared towards children let alone children with sensory processing difficulties. In the end, I decided to purchase a drawing pad and ask him to draw his feelings about starting his second year in middle school. I thought to myself that this could be the ice breaker we needed to get to the root cause(s) behind his increased level of anxiety. *Fingers crossed* is what I kept telling myself, *fingers crossed*.

And then it happened. The last day in August was business night at middle school. It's the time when students get their schedules for the year and meet their teachers. Everything seemed really cool the days leading up to business night. My son was extremely excited about being a seventh grader. There were times when he asked me if I thought he was nervous but when I asked him if he was, he always told me no. I knew the anxiety was the norm as although he was attending the same school it still was another transition.

Oh man, I had no idea how high his anxiety levels were until we pulled into the school's parking lot. He kept repeating himself, "Do you think I'm nervous, do you think I'm nervous?" No matter how many times I tried to calm his fears you could see the anxiety welling up in his belly. He really feared making the transition to seventh grade.

When we walked into the school building, he spoke to a few kids he met last school year. It seemed to be okay until we, rather I, entered the room with several parents and students in it. I looked around and couldn't find my child anywhere. As I walked further out of the classroom door, I noticed that he had hidden behind the door of another classroom. It took me several tries to convince him that it was okay to enter the room. All I kept thinking was how in the world would he manage the first day of school?

By the end of the tour, he was a little more at ease when he saw his former gym teacher. It seemed like a weight had been lifted off his shoulders and everything was okay. I decided to allow him to draw out his feelings as sometimes feelings can be messy for him to handle. Through his drawing he told me that he felt shy about starting the seventh grade. I really hoped that his shyness would gradually go away as school would be starting soon and I wanted him to be the best seventh grader that he could possibly be. Cheers to the first month of the new school year.

We're officially at the end of the first month of school. I think the newness of seventh grade has worn off and old habits are creeping up again. I'm assuming they were reviewing sixth grade materials as now those As and Bs are slowly becoming Fs again. The excuses are returning as well as the blame game. *The teacher doesn't like me*, or *the teacher is being rude to me* are now reasons for not returning school assignments or refusing to study at home. Hello young man, there aren't enough minutes in the day for you to study for ALL your classes during homeroom. Where are your books? *My teacher let me study in his/her classroom*. Better yet, *Umm what book was that for again?* I really don't understand how this work nowadays. I'm sure I made excuses for missing assignments every now and then. However, this is a daily event in my home and seemed to get worse after fifth grade.

Is it executive functioning issues? Is it the Autism? Or is it just that he's just uninterested in school? It's probably a combination of both as in the minds of some teens school is simply boring. They're more invested in socializing and building networks and less on spending quality time in the books. It's even harder when your child struggles to organize and plan his thoughts let alone execute those plans that seem to be scattered all over the place.

I've decided this school year that I'm not going to bail him out by sending emails to his classroom teachers every time I see a low score. It's going to be tough as I want him to perform well in school. However, it's more important to me that he learns how to self-advocate for himself since I won't be alive forever. Scary thought I know but it's the truth. He must want to be successful for himself and not to please me. I've always told my children that if you earn an F, earn it because you worked your tail off and not because you failed to study. Every failure can lead to an opportunity for greater success if you choose to refocus and try even harder the second, third, or 80th time around.

Well, after that conversation we had after several eye rolls, yes mamas, and requests to draw me pictures; I feel like it was one sided as in the end his responses were either *Can you take me out of xyz class* or *I'm not good in xyz class.* Calgon take me away as this was only the first month of school. We must shift gears soon otherwise we will be where we were at the end of last school year—rushing to redo large amounts of assignments to improve his overall grades. It was emotionally and mentally stressful for the both of us and I'm just not interested in doing it another year.

Did I say I wasn't doing it again?

I won't say that I lied but what I will say is that I'm doing a modified version of where we were last year. It took every ounce of restraint not to email his teachers about what he needs to be successful this school year. Instead I decided to place the ball back in his court, so to speak, and focus on his end goals for the first nine weeks. Score!

    I said score because what I realized is that arguing back and forth with my son was getting us nowhere. He is extremely literal and if you want him to act on important information you must firmly state it first and leave the extra verbiage behind. For example, he earned a score of zero on an assignment as he stated that the teacher told the students that they weren't required to turn it in. He never did. Well he was 100% correct as the information stated on the parent website indicated that the students were not required to turn it in. However, they were required to show the assignment to the teacher to receive full credit. So, depending on which statement the teacher used first, don't turn it in but show me or vice versa, my son only heard the initial statement and not the rest. Wow!

    Now that I changed the narrative for him and showed him how showing his teacher his assignment would boost his overall grade from a D to a B, buy-in had been secured. How did I know this? Prior to going to bed I asked him what he was required to provide his teacher upon entering the classroom. Not only did he share with me the necessary steps he should take but also what it would mean for his overall grade and earning his end of the first nine weeks reward.

    There's a part of me that still wants to write the email. However, if my goal is to teach my son how to self-advocate, I'll have to give him space and not overshadow him. If he doesn't do it after being given the opportunity, we will write an email together to his teacher asking for permission to bring it in the following day. This is going to be a learning curve for me as parent and school psychologist, but it must be done.

    Let the learning curve begin as the start of this school year will be a roller coaster ride it, seems, with hormones kicking in and him simply being a tween.

The school year has progressed and as a family we are finally getting into a groove with school. Our routine is established, and all is well in our world. We're still working on verbally self-advocating but so far, knock on wood, there has been only a few occasions when emails have been sent regarding missing assignments. The phrase *I know, mom* has become popular these days.

This really is an exciting year it seems like for my son. He's excited about going to school and speaks highly of most teachers. My son even shared that he had, yes had, a girlfriend. For parents of children with ASD social relationships and social acceptance are two areas of difficulty. The fact that he had a girlfriend created a lot of excitement for me as my son was finally being socially accepted by his peers now more than ever.

Like I said before, my son had a girlfriend at the beginning of the school year. However, maybe it was around the fourth or fifth week into the school year that my son told me that they'd broken up. I was crushed when I heard the news as his girlfriend seemed to bring out the best in him. For example, he smiled more and was more open to share with me all the cool things (i.e. walking her to class) they would do together at school. Now as we all know, there are three sides to every story, your side, my side, and the truth. I only had one side of the story, which was his. According to my son, one day his girlfriend refused to call their teacher by her proper name. When both my son and the teacher tried to correct her, the young lady refused. He shared he had to break up with her because she made a bad choice and was being rude, in his opinion, to the teacher. It really didn't bother him much, but I was still very sad as this was the first time he acknowledged having a girlfriend.I know, I know, school is meant for learning and not for dating. However, positive relationships whether it be with peers or teachers are important in helping students have a healthy school experience. Unfortunately, when some students do not have positive relationships at school, their work productivity and motivation to learn and perform may be impacted.

As a parent and educator, I know that having the right teacher alignment is key with students if we want to see them rise to their full academic and behavioral potentials. All seemed well at the start of the new school year and then began to ever so slightly change after the first interim report. As a parent I initially thought that either my son wasn't putting forth the effort to perform or that the classes were so heavily language loaded that it made it more challenging for him to keep up with the pace. Sigh. Since I will be honest, I felt like he wasn't putting forth much effort as he would never ask for help at home and would always state that he completed his work in class. I remember scolding him for not doing his best as this was his pattern last school year.

Lesson learned. The past is just that, the past. Never use it as a marker for what will be in the present moment or the future.

Yet the grades continued to decline. I just couldn't understand it. In other classes that were heavily language loaded he excelled. I just convinced myself that he performed better in those classes as activities were highly visual and there were a lot of hands-on tasks that could be given to facilitate learning. There was something missing in this equation and I just couldn't figure it out.

I decided to reach out to my son's case manager to find out if it would be possible to assist him during his resource time as it made a difference last school year. The response I received was shocking. Not only was my child in classes with a teacher that he struggled to get along with the previous school year, BUT he wasn't receiving his resource time as written in his individualized education plan (IEP).

What? I had so many questions and concerns running through my head when I received this news including the fact that there were only a few weeks left before the first nine-week grading period ended.

The first and most important question I had was WHY. Why was my son placed in a class, let me correct this, classes with a teacher that he struggled with the prior school year? Why wasn't a meeting called within the first two weeks of school to discuss his schedule and his IEP as they weren't aligned? Why did I not see these things happening? Why didn't my son tell me that he was not being pulled for his resource time? Why? Why? Why?

Honestly, I have no clue how or why the ball was dropped at the school level as most of the information regarding my son's educational needs and relationships with specific teachers had been documented the previous year. Like so many parents, I entrusted that my child's school would have rechecked his schedule just like the other students to ensure that it aligned with his IEP. I get it. Middle school caseloads are HUGE depending on the school size. However, when a child is not making solid progress, a team meeting should have been called to reassess the IEP especially if resource time is clearly written on the IEP.

After fuming and emotionally feeling defeated, I contacted the school to request that an emergency IEP meeting be held as the school was in violation of his IEP and to discuss his issues with one teacher. The school accommodated my request and the meeting was held the following week. As a group, we looked at the missteps that were made and how to best support my son moving forward. It was a happy and sad occasion for me. On one hand, I was happy that he would be receiving his resource services as my child really respects his case manager and she him. Their relationship is one of trust and open communication, which as a parent is all that I could ever want or ask for in his teacher. I was sad as he would no longer be receiving intensive reading supports to address his new diagnosis of dyslexia. When I mentioned this at the meeting, his case manager heard my fears and placed interventions in place to address his reading delays during his resource time. She also agreed that both she and her assistant would serve in rotation in those two classes where my son was underperforming. Since the shift was made, he went from underperforming in those two classes to earning average scores by the end of the first nine-week period. Positive relationships matter for children, especially those with ASD.

I know there is still more that will happen this school year but for now our family has a routine that works, and my son is happy about being in school.

SOCIAL ACCEPTANCE OR REJECTION

Friends or frenemies? This is the million-dollar question that we all will face throughout our life's journey as adults. Children and adolescents are no exception to this question as social engagement and learning social rules occur everywhere including classrooms, school bus stops, the playground, etc. However, it is often difficult to determine if the intention on the part of the individual befriending you is positive or negative. For individuals with ASD, their inability to read and understand social cues makes it even more challenging for them to determine if a person is truly a friend or a frenemy.

Social acceptance and rejection as adolescents is at an all-time high as peer relationships become more important to them. During this phase in children's lives, they are often questioning how and when their peers are evaluating everything they say and do. The perceived evaluations of others in turn may positively or negatively influence the emotional intensity and social behaviors adolescents display from one day to the next (Somerville, 2013). Now imagine what this may look like for a child who already struggles with understanding social cues. Is he or she truly able to evaluate how his or her peers are evaluating him or her? Will the inability to interpret social idioms due to seeing everything as black or white impede their ability to respond in a socially appropriate manner?

I think so as this seems to be an ongoing pattern not only for my child but for children I've worked with throughout my career. I wish I'd had umbrellas every time I saw a parent cry during a meeting as they shared their stories or as I internally cried as I'm thinking to myself *I get it*. I hear you. I sympathize with you. If we lived in a world where differences were celebrated I think our world would be a much happier place. I need to refocus now as my eyes are beginning to mist a little while typing this section. Just know that I get it! I feel your pain! Different is unique and is not often accepted by others.

When it comes to social acceptance, my son is no different. He wants to fit in so badly with his typical peers as intrinsically he knows that his behaviors and communication skills are not at the same level as his peers. Unfortunately, his need for social acceptance has gotten him into a few issues this school year. I can think of a time in our life when my son wanted a video game badly. He asked for it constantly as it was a must-have. As parents, his father and I have always agreed that the majority of gifts of love that we provide to our children will always be what they need, and one would be something that they really wanted. The gift was purchased and the excitement in his eyes upon receiving it was electrifying. I knew he wanted the game, which is why his actions were quite unnerving to me.

Without boring you with all the details, let's just say that one minute the game was in the home and then four days AFTER he last played with the game, it was gone! Are you kidding me? I was upset on that day since I knew he took the game to school to share with friends AFTER talking about it with them. However, the tales that were told was maddening in my head. One minute he lost it and it could never be found. Then he said that he'd given it away and that he could never get it back. Another story shared was that it was in his locker. No matter the tales he told, both his father and I agreed that the game needed to be returned home in the same condition it was taken out of the house. He lost everything on that day and he was devastated as he couldn't understand what he'd done wrong.

In hindsight, I believe that my son like any child was trying to prove that he was just as cool as his typical peers.

The reality is that my son has semi-embraced the fact that he has ASD. In his mind, he is ASD when he goes to the resource classroom or when he's at home and that's cool. However, at school, he just wants to be accepted like everyone else. This often brings me to tears as children with ASD are targets for bullying as they have the tendency to be socially naïve compared to their more socially savvy peers (Altomare et al., 2017).

The social naivete finally became evident during my son's seventh grade year. Unfortunately, there was a point in time in my son's life when he became the victim of bullying.

Before I share his story, I want to be very clear. Regardless if your child is the bully, bystander, or victim, bullying is a serious issue in our society. No matter where you look, whether it's turning on the TV, witnessing domestic aggression (verbal and/or physical) within one's home, or at school, children are being exposed to bullying on a regular basis. If our society does not get a handle on this issue, the level of emotional trauma in children will increase exponentially.

Let me refocus at this point as it's one thing when you hear about bullying issues happening to the children of family members and friends. It's another issue when it happens to your own child.

Children with ASD often struggle with establishing appropriate peer relationships due to difficulties understanding nonverbal cues. Those with higher functioning autism, formally known as Asperger's Disorder, also have difficulties with social idioms. For example, if one were to say, *Button your lips*, most individuals would understand this phrase to mean be quiet. Since individuals with high functioning Autism are literal they may look at the speaker inquisitively and make comments to respond to the speaker's statement (e.g. I don't have a button on my lip). An inability to understand social idioms unfortunately make children with ASD more susceptible to bullying.

Social stories are often used to teach individuals with ASD how to interact with peers and adults. Many of these stories are related to what is happening in children's lives to assist them in navigating their school environments. This was no different for my child as his stories always reflected his responses to individuals (i.e. using kind words instead of mean words). He learned these lessons and for the most part implemented them at school and home since he was in elementary school.

Yet something shifted in his behaviors his seventh grade year. I noticed that he was becoming more aggressive towards his younger brother again, which had been curtailed for several months since he began therapy. He seemed to be a little moodier than normal. I simply associated it with being a tween and left it at that.

One day I received an urgent text from my mom that there was some yelling at the bus stop across the street from our house. There was swearing and my seventh grader was involved. When I returned home from work, I asked my son what was going on and he said *nothing*. When I told him that it was okay to share, he expressed that certain students on the bus were picking on him. In my head, I questioned if they were really picking on him or was he struggling to pick up social cues within his environment and assumed that these students were picking on him? We processed it out and indeed my son believed that these individuals were saying mean things to him.

The teasing seemed to stop as my son didn't comment on the subject matter again. However, I had to realize that my son is the type of child who seeks to please adults and if he perceives that his actions or words will disappoint them, he will "fake good." It's a term used in psychology to reflect that people will provide an individual with a desired response that they expect the other person would want from them or they simply want to make others believe that everything is positive so that they too may be viewed in a positive light. I wouldn't ask him often, but I did ask.

Then it happened again. More cussing and fussing as the students exited the school bus. I received another text from my mom and this time my son appeared to be visibly shaken up by this event. When I came home, my son and I processed this out and initially he didn't want to share with me what happened. Eventually he did and apparently the children were asking him questions about me that my son didn't like. When I asked him if that were everything, he said no as one of the children indicated that he had planned to fight him the next day. I decided at that point to reach out to the administration at the school as I knew that the administration was responsible for all locations during school hours including the school bus stop.

Nothing. Nada. No response back. I know that administrators have time off during the weekend, so I was not expecting to receive any feedback. However, if an email is sent on a Friday with the subject line to include the word *bullying*, one would expect that a reply would be sent sometime during that day. Nada. Nothing at all.

A new school week began and this time I decided to start my day a little earlier so that I could monitor my son's actions as he was still concerned about getting into a fight. I vividly remembered my son pacing back and forth on the side of the road next to the bus stop as the students approached the area. A few words were exchanged, the students including my son looked to see who was watching, and it seemed like everything calmed down. I thought in my head, *Maybe I'll start my day earlier so that he won't get into any more altercations as he had in his past.*

Now I've heard those complaints before about parents

expressing concerns related to bullying in school with no response from administrators. However, like other parents, I'd hoped that would not have been in our case especially with the rise in suicide among young people to date because of school and cyber bullying issues. At that point, I decided to ask others how they dealt with issues related to bullying before something worse happened.

Well the worst did happen. On the evening prior to the event, my son asked me if he could use some of his earned money to buy a cookie at school. I told him yes as he'd been doing well at school and did an excellent job not getting into any fights at the bus stop. It was a well-deserved reward.

The next day he reminded me about getting his money and I acknowledged his request again. As he prepared to go to the bus stop, he was running a little behind schedule, so the other children were already walking to the stop. My son seemed okay leaving the house and left a little before I walked out the door. My mom was watching out the door as normal. Suddenly she opened the door and yelled, "Hey." I immediately turned around to see my son handing over his cookie money to the child who he previously said wanted to fight him. I yelled "Put that money back in your bag. It's for lunch." Both boys looked at me, with the other student immediately handing the money back to my son.

Immediately I'd assumed that my son was giving him the money for one of two reasons. First, I thought he did it as he wanted to be socially accepted and felt like giving him the money was his way to "pay" the other student to like him. Then I thought maybe the boy had wanted a cookie at school and didn't have any money, so my son was giving him the money to help him out. Not matter the reason, the money was given back.

Then I received another text from my mom because there were more verbal issues after the children returned home. This time when I spoke with my son and asked him to tell me the truth, he shared that he took the money with him so that he would not be beaten up by the other student. When I clarified my son's concerns, he repeated the same statement. I was fuming once again as I still had not received any response from administration regarding my first complaint and now three school days after my first event, another issue occurred. I immediately sent off an email requesting more information regarding the school district's policy regarding bullying in exchange for money.

The more I thought about the situation, the angrier I became as I questioned that if the first email had been responded to this other event may not have occurred. Without going into a lot of details as there will be a separate book focusing on knowing your rights in relation to bullying issues in your state, I reported this issue to the school as well as the local authority. In the end, as in most complaints related to bullying at school, his case was dismissed.

Deflated, yes. Defeated, no. After realizing that the school would not take action regarding my child's case, I decided to start taking him to school. There was nothing I could do in the afternoon as I had to be at work. However, since most of the issues began in the morning and trickled down into the afternoon bus ride, I decided that if I eliminated the morning issues the afternoon ones would subside. I also shared my concerns with my son's therapist and she too agreed that this was in his best interest. As an educator, I know the effects of bullying all too well and my concern was related to my son's overall emotional and mental health statuses. According to a recent study completed by Tsaousis (2016) "Children and adolescents who are bullied are at increased risk for mental health problems" (p. 186). With so many heartbreaking stories of young people committing suicide due to school or cyber bullying, I didn't want my son to be one of the statistics. Only time will tell if this was the best course of action for my son. I just hope this experience doesn't change his happy go lucky personality.

WHEN THE FLOOD RAGES: WHAT NEXT?

Parents of children with ASD are familiar with the fact that our babies struggle to regulate their emotions for one reason or another. Whether it be sound, light, or texture, their ability to process sensory information seems to be all over the place.

I am all too familiar with this as my son has had sensory issues since age 2. He tends to focus on one part of the room as he hums and jumps to release the pent-up energy that seems to consume him. Once he has released this energy, he becomes calmer and is more manageable.

There have been times in his earlier years where his difficulty in processing information from his environment has caused him to find himself in hot water at school. Whether it be hitting a peer, throwing a shoe at a teacher, or eloping, my son has always found a way to escape when things were too much for him to handle.

I had grown used to the mini-fights and had even had it pinned down to one season, spring time, per year. However, as he got older and the demands at school increased, the seasons were no longer relevant. When things didn't feel right in his environment he would lash out.

As I previously shared at the beginning, my child has had several suspensions throughout his school career primarily starting in 5th grade. Don't get me wrong—he was asked not to return to one preschool and had a half day suspension in second grade. However, the older he became the more frequent the calls.

As a mom, having the school call my cellphone so much was annoying at times even as an educator. I know that the schools are only doing their job by removing the student from the situation or finding out the root cause of what leads to a student's inappropriate behavior(s). However, the more the calls came, the more I became numb. I didn't want to deal with the calls any longer as it seemed like there wasn't anything positive they shared about my child. Or maybe they did share some positive words but the initial conversation of "Hi, Dr. Lisbon, this is so and so. We have your child sitting with us in the office again." Again? Again? How many times would he be in the office again before they could figure out what was triggering these behaviors?

Am I the only mother who has felt this overwhelmed by these phone calls? Don't get me wrong—I knew that my son had anger problems that from time to time would get the best of him at home. However, it was not to the degree that, in my opinion, the schools were making it out to be.

I remember many days when parents at my schools would echo these same words in meetings. "Is it really all that?" or "Do these people not realize I have to work?" For me it became, do these individuals know that every time they call me I feel like I am not doing my job as his mother to meet his basic needs?

Let me clarify my point so that you won't think that my son was in trouble every single day. My son was suspended a lot less than many of my students with ASD or with other disorders. However, I just didn't like how I felt when they called. Here I was, the school psychologist, providing strategies and resources to help parents and teachers support the needs of students with disabilities at my school buildings and yet I didn't have a handle on my own child's behaviors. Truthfully, anything would set my son off, but it seemed to get worse during the tween years.

Hormones, hormones, go away. I really dislike this cat and mouse game you play. As my son has gotten older, the hormones are kicking in and I know that he's struggling to understand these feelings along with his Autism. I remember speaking with a former occupational therapist colleague when he was 11 years old and she shared with me that his aggression may increase a little more do to his inability to deal with all the hormone changes he was undergoing. I thought I knew what to expect but I didn't at all.

It was the weekend and the weather was nice. Everything was calm, and everyone seemed to be at peace. Let me preface by saying that maybe I should have picked my battle with this situation. However, when I gave him several opportunities to tell the truth and the only responses were lies, I had to stand firm in my position so that my son understood that lying was not okay.

As always, trying to figure out what triggers an individual with ASD is like trying to find a needle in a haystack. It's challenging as one minute you think that you've found what causes a meltdown and the next minute you find out it's something brand new. I wish there were a crystal ball or some type of "what to expect when your ASD child has a meltdown" book so that I could read up on and learn how to respond better in situations.

Like for most moms, our children's triggers can occur at any time, any place, and with anyone. Would you agree with this? On this particular weekend, I can recall that his meltdown occurred during a warm day in January. I should have known that the day would be awry as we were in the dead of winter and it felt like spring. Not a good sign. Not a good sign at all.

I thought the whole event started when I expressed to my son that he should not accept a snack if he knew he had no intentions of eating it. I even offered him the opportunity to try it as I knew that he didn't like things with a cheese flavor. When he accepted the snack, he was told that he was required to eat it. Long story short, he pretended to eat a few. When I told him to go back and finish the rest, he pretended as though he gulped it down within two minutes. Now I wasn't a fool as three-fourths of the bowl was filled with the snack. Yet he argued with me that he had eaten it all. When none of the children would 'fess up as to where the snack went, I assigned an earlier bed time for everyone. Oh, my word! Who told me to do this? My son was very upset and continued to assert that he had eaten the snack. I had given him several options to comply with my request. Even with giving him multiple compromises, he wanted it his way or no way.

He eventually went into his room as he normally would to calm down. Suddenly, he began screaming in the bathroom and then ran into my room. My son continued to beg and plead with me that if he didn't have his way, he would act out in school the next day. I shared with him that if he chose to make bad choices, he would have to accept consequences from school and at home. I assume that he thought I would change my position after he continued stating that he would get into fights at school or curse at school authority. I continued to remind him that his choices would lead to his consequences. It was dead silence thereafter. Or so I thought.

It seemed like this had been going on for hours, but it was more like 15 or 20 minutes. He even threatened to pack his suitcases and move out of the house. I politely reminded him that he needed a plan and funding to move anywhere else so that was out of the question. He was required to find another solution.

Suddenly, we were at a standstill as he continued to rant wildly about his intentions at school the next day. When I was at my wits' end, I finally yelled "That's enough." This appeared to infuriate him, because it wasn't enough for him as he hadn't won the "match."

Eventually, the name calling and swearing started. I had gotten used to the name calling and even the swearing as I've had it happen to me at work with students who were enraged as well as my son on a few rare occasions. No harm, no foul I assumed.

Yet the rage in his eyes began to consume him and for the first time EVER in my life, my child, my first born, had indicated that he wanted to physically harm me. He was so enraged that he kept looking for weapons to carry out his threat. I knew this was not his intent as he had several opportunities to get a weapon and lunge towards me. The fact that he used those words crushed my spirit as it was then that I realized the true power ASD has over individuals. I wasn't afraid of him per se but I felt powerless as I know that my son is a good child who wouldn't harm anyone unless he felt threatened or afraid. However, the child that stood in front of me wasn't MY son as MY son, MY boy would never want to hurt me. He has always been over protective of me, which is why I felt powerless in this situation as I wasn't reaching my baby.

Imagine what it's like to be unable to identify your feelings in words. Imagine being in such a defense mode that you no longer have control of your body. Imagine what it's like, if you haven't experienced it already, what it's like to hear your child say, "Surrender or die." It seemed like time had frozen for a moment and I was reliving the stories that my parents would share in meetings regarding their own children. I would always think this could never happen to me as I was a trained professional and had worked with children with ASD for many years. However, as I am always reminded, it's one thing to work with a child at school as there are a lot of social pressures that are at stake in trying to fit in and be "normal." It's something different when you are at home and those social pressures no longer exist.

April J. Lisbon

I just wanted this moment to end. I wanted to go back in time, earlier in the day when everything was peaceful, and all was right in our home. Unfortunately, this was not the case and I would have never imagined that I would hear these words from my child, but I did. It scared me—he was a tween. It scared me because his siblings heard these words. It scared me that if this had happened anyplace else other than at home, he may have been arrested or even worse. I didn't want to think of what else might have happened if his rage continued to brew. Rather than take any additional chances, I decided to call our local non-emergency number to provide support within our home. I literally had to remove my two youngest children from the home while my mom cornered him to one side of the living room as we waited for someone from the sheriff's office to arrive at our home.

I was heartbroken that the call had been made. Yet the rage was too great, and I had to protect myself and the other children from his fury. My mom did a great job praying with him, which seemed to help. By the time the deputies arrived, he was calm enough to speak with one of them. Initially, he was afraid to say anything because he was a Black male speaking to a White law enforcement agent. When I explained to him that speaking to this officer was no different than speaking with the deputies we had spoken with during the time he was bullied earlier in the school year, he did his best to communicate what had happened. By the end of the event, we all agreed that having him speak with someone at the local hospital would be in his best interest to help him regulate even more. The officer asked me if he was calm enough to drive in my vehicle, which I said that he was. We went to the hospital and he was so remorseful for what he had done. He knew the decision that he had made was not in his best interest; yet he didn't know how to "shut off'" the anger.

As a parent and educator, I too had no idea on how to shut off this level of anger and aggression as it was brand new to me. He had never displayed this type of aggression that I was aware of at home, even when he was mad with his siblings or even me. I am sure a lot of this is related to hormones and just maturing. The challenging of authority comes with the territory with any tween or teen. Heck, even we as adults will challenge authority from time to time. Yet in this moment, I realized that ASD was much greater than I was, and no amount of degrees and professional experiences prepared me for this day. I hope and pray that it will never be at this level again. For several days after this event, I was extremely exhausted. I felt like I wasn't getting enough sleep or maybe I simply wasn't sleeping well. My energy level was zapped and my tank was running well below E. All in all, what I do know is this one thing—IF this should ever happen again, I pray that we will both pick our battles and simply let go when things become too heated. I never want to make that call again as that was the hardest thing I've ever had to do as a mother.

Words of Inspiration

This Autism lifestyle is filled with so many twists and turns that will cause you to question your sanity as well as your ability to move forward on this journey. Depending on the length or intensity of your child's meltdowns or explosive fits of rage, it may leave you mentally, physically, and emotionally exhausted. Yet I want to leave you all with words of inspiration knowing that you can and will survive this journey.

Will it be hard? Absolutely. But it will be worth it all in the end as you are a great mother.

So, in this last section of this book before I close out, I want to offer each of you four words of encouragement to help you on this ASD journey. Those words are: *hope*, *faith*, *peace*, and *perseverance*. We need all four to strengthen us when life seems unfair and is not going our way. Practice care of self so that you can care for your child. Never allow your tank to become empty as it will only make your fight less manageable.

Keep up the good fight of faith! Let's start with H-O-P-E.

Before you start reading each section below, I want you to really meditate on what each word means to you. Don't rush through this process as you want to build a foundation for yourself so in those moments when you feel like your child is on the brink of an explosion or you are on the brink of an explosion, you can take the time to think about the real meanings of hope, faith, peace, and perseverance in your life. If it takes you one hour, one day, or even one week, meditate on these words until they are imprinted into your hearts and minds.

Once you have done this, breathe and read each section slowly. Then take the time to use the pages that have been provided and any other pages you need to write your most authentic thoughts regarding these words. Writing things down helps you keep a record of a time when you were at your most peaceful state. Think of it as your intimate staycation.

You may now begin this process of discovery as you write down your thoughts on your journey through *Autism in April*.

Hope

"Hope fills the holes of my frustration in my heart."
—Emanuel Cleaver

As you embark on your journey as a parent of a child with special needs, never give up hope no matter how frustrating or unfair this life may seem. There is something within you that has the power to transform the world and it is through your pain that you will find your true purpose in life.

Our children with special needs have gifted us with the ability to FEEL fear, FACE fear, and FIGHT fear. I cannot tell you how many times I've wanted to give up on this journey as it's hard. The grief, the shame, and the pain has often become unbearable from time to time. There have been many days I've asked myself am I really built for THIS lifestyle? Do I really have what it takes to be the mother of a child with ASD? Can I give my son ALL that he needs without losing sight of me?

And the answer is a resounding YES. Yes, I can be a good mother to my son because I am his biggest supporter and advocate. Yes, I was built for this lifestyle as if God or whomever you denote as your higher power did not believe that I had the "goods" to take care of my son then he may have been blessed to be given to another family. But the only way I can be the best I can be for him is that I must start taking care of myself.

It's not enough to have hope if you're running on fumes from day to day. Hope is a noun and a verb. As a noun it plays on your feelings and emotions of, for example, desiring that something will happen. As a verb you're activating your desire that something will happen. The same is true when you are caring for a child with special needs. It is not enough that you have feelings that one day you'll find time to care for yourself as you care for your child or children with special needs. When will you or how have you ACTIVATED your desire to care for yourself while caring for your child?

Recently, I decided to practice self-care through taking long hot baths. Everyone including my child with ASD has learned that once they hear the jazz music in the bathroom area on my side of the house, it's mommy time. They've also learned that once the music stops, it's their time.

I've also found a hobby that I really enjoyed after desperately seeking the perfect one. It's writing. I try to write one page a day to release the emotions, positive or negative, that I am feeling while challenging myself to find one solution to help feed my heart, mind, and soul with positive energy. Words of affirmation have been powerful in helping me find hope on those days when I find myself being discouraged on this ASD journey. Creating balance is one key to ensuring that you have hope for tomorrow.

Just know that it's okay to FEEL the FEAR. Just don't COMMIT to the FEAR. Fear is normal as we are unsure of what may happen tomorrow. However, once you acknowledge the fear, let it go by activating your faith. Trust that you have what it takes to be the parent of a child with special needs!

AUTISM IN APRIL

My hope is…

April J. Lisbon

AUTISM IN APRIL

April J. Lisbon

Faith

"Sometimes life hits you in the head with a brick. Don't lose faith."
—Steve Jobs

Faith is the opposite of fear in that you are believing and/or hoping for something to happen even when you are unable to visualize the outcome. As a parent of children with ASD or maybe it's just me, I find myself walking on shaky faith as there are times on this journey where my son is doing well behaviorally and emotionally. It seems like his sensory needs are "reducing" along with his levels of anxiety. And then bam, just like a brick hitting me on top of my head, it hurts. The words, the aggression, the lying, everything hurts and seems to come out of nowhere. It's a daily struggle parenting a child with ASD as there are times when I'm unsure which one of my child's moods will appear first—happy, sad, angry, or indifferent. But I keep moving forward!

I've learned to move forward as I realized that my son needs me to remain a foundation of stabilization for him. Because he sometimes feels disconnected from himself and his ASD, he needs me to remain rooted in this process of not giving up on him and not giving up on our journey. It takes a lot of daily faith for me to do this as I'm unsure how much more I can take as I too feel like I'm becoming unglued.

What do you hope for? Where does your faith come from? Is it the universe, the divine, God? Who or what have you planted your faith in to help you on your ASD journey? Find your higher calling and purpose on this journey as there is a purpose for everything that we experience as ASD mommies. Whether it be to write books, share our stories on stages, or to hold another mother who has a child with ASD or another disability, there is purpose in this process we are undertaking.

As I write this book, I am in the process of helping other families of children with special needs as an author, family coach, and empowerment speaker. If you would have told me this back in mid-2017, I would have said no as I was still uncomfortable about sharing my journey as a mom of a child with ASD for fear of how others would perceive me and my son. I am a true mama bear and will protect my cubs at all cost so to expose parts of our life's journey simply didn't feel good.

When I finally stopped focusing on me and more about those I could help, I decided to activate my faith level and publish my first book. It was so freeing to know that in being transparent I had the potential to support families I know and those I'd never meet.

Begin to activate your faith. Never give up on the possibilities of seeing your child succeed in this life. Even when the clouds come, and the tears fall, trust that you know what you are doing in this process. No one is perfect and we all make mistakes. It's in your imperfections that if you don't give up, you'll walk this journey in faith and find peace in the middle of your storm.

Have faith and NEVER give up!

I have faith that...

April J. Lisbon

AUTISM IN APRIL

April J. Lisbon

Peace

"To discover your mission and put it into action—instead of worrying on the sidelines—is to find peace of mind and a heart full of love."
—Scilla Elworthy

As mothers we have dreams and visions for our children to excel in every area of life. We want them to be the best persons they can be even better than us. However, this lived experiences of parenting a child or children with ASD can deflate or even downright take away those dreams and visions we have.

Mom, you have every right to feel this way as for so many years society has shined a light that being "different" is strange or just wrong. This only sets in more worry that your child or children will not be accepted by others. Guess what? You are probably correct in how you are feeling, and I want you to embrace those feelings. However, as I said before do not commit yourself to these feelings as you do not want them to consume your mind and your heart.

My hope for each of you reading this book is that as you discover your purpose on this journey of parenting a child with ASD is that you'll realize you will find the peace of mind you so desperately need to walk this lifestyle out. I want you to speak life into your heart and mind and say daily "I am more than enough." I want you to tell yourself daily "Although it hurts me today, I am growing through this process and one day from now, one month from now, one year from now. No matter what, I am growing." We must speak positive words of affirmations so that we do not spiral out of control. As I learned on a speaking tour, the only way you can truly understand and embrace the purpose of your pain is through the process of self-discovery (Anderson-Abram, 2018). Whether this discovery comes through coaching, counseling, or in-depth introspection, just know that you are positioned to succeed on this journey because of who you are as a person.

I remind myself daily that I will no longer allow the stress and pressures of raising a child with ASD consume me. Do I cry? Yes. Am I angry? Yes. Will I give up? Never as I realize that this was the assignment that was given to me by the Creator and it is my duty as my son's mother to create balance in his life and that of my other children. The only way I can create this balance is if my heart and mind agree that I can do this.

What are you willing to do today to discover your mission and put it into action? How will you develop self-care skills that will motivate you to worry less and no longer sit on the sidelines of this journey we call Autism? The power lies in you. Find your superpower and let it guide you until you find peace in every area of your life.

You can do this, moms! YOU CAN DO THIS!

AUTISM IN APRIL

I give myself permission to be in a state of peacefulness...

April J. Lisbon

AUTISM IN APRIL

April J. Lisbon

Perseverance

"I learned patience, perseverance, and dedication. Now I really know myself, and I know my voice. It's a voice of pain and victory."
— *Anthony Hamilton*

Keep on moving! I've said it before, I'll say it again, this journey that we are undertaking can be darn right exhausting. Some days are better than other days though. Even yesterday as I took a mental break from writing, I realized that I had to move past the pain, the what-ifs, and any other roadblocks that I could think of that could stop me from telling this story. Being an ASD mother is hard.

I found this quote to be personally inspirational as I have the tendency to be impatient when things aren't going according to plan. This journey has tested my patience on SO many levels that I have no clue how I've "stayed in the ring" this long.

I've always known that I was a strong person as throughout my lifetime I've overcome many hurdles that people have questioned how I made it. There are times when I look back on my life prior to having children, that I too question how I overcame those hurdles as the pressure and pain while going through them was too much to bear in real time. Yet I did.

How about you, mom? Can you think of some pains that you went through prior to being a mom that you ask yourself—hey, how did I make it? I'm sure you can as we all have many stories that we can share. It's because we all persevered. There was something deep down inside of us that just wouldn't allow us to give in or give up on ourselves. Whether it is the Creator, the Divine, or your higher power, it helped you get up, dust yourself off, and continue your life's path. Personally, I think all the obstacles that I overcame throughout my life helped prepared me for this ASD lifestyle as I would always complain that the pain was too unbearable and there wasn't any way I could survive anything more. Well, I did—we did. For me I truly believe that I needed those experiences to help me realize that I could be victorious no matter what life threw at me, even if the hurt and pains were directed towards my children. I knew how pain felt BUT I also knew what it meant to overcome those pains. As I've said before, I was built for this ASD lifestyle.

In the end, what I've come to terms with is that I consciously chose to dedicate myself to walking this journey out with my son as he didn't choose to be on the Autism Spectrum. This was the life that he was given and as his mother I want to help him as best as I know how. He sees me as his solid foundation where he can plant himself when the weight of his world is more than he can bear. Is it painful for the two of us to be at odds? Absolutely. Is it painful to watch my son continue to experience the residual effects of being bullied months after it occurred? Absolutely. Is it painful to hear my son state that he hates school because it's too hard for him? Absolutely. Yet I am committed to moving my son past his own hurts and pains to ensure that he becomes a productive member of his community as he grows older.Let your voice be heard. You are much stronger than you'll ever know so continue to move forward and persevere!

AUTISM IN APRIL

I will persevere...

April J. Lisbon

AUTISM IN APRIL

April J. Lisbon

Final Thoughts

As mothers we all have hopes and big dreams for our children from the time that we conceive. We think about their personalities, their hopes and dreams, and being the best mother we can be for them. When you hold your children in your arms for the first time, you make promises to shield and protect them from harm that may come their way while they're here on earth.

Yet you never planned to be the parent of a child with special needs. You never planned for your child to be diagnosed with ASD. It was never in the plan but it's your life story.

I want to encourage everyone of you reading this book that your life's story of raising a child with special needs is one of resilience. It's one of finding hope and promises in areas where the world and others may find it hopeless. It's one of tears. It's one of growth. It's one of strength. It's one of pain. But it's YOUR story. Never allow the pressures of this journey to redefine who you are as a woman and as a mother. If you weren't strong enough to handle this journey, the universe would have never gifted you with your child or children with special needs.

Find time to love and embrace yourself as a woman first and then as a mother. Take time to practice daily self-care whether it be listening to calming music, finding time to take a soaking bath, or reading a good book. Take time to ground yourself and create a level of stabilization that your child with ASD needs to feel secure in his/her physical being. When we as mothers are calm, our children become calm. Is this easy? No but it's worth practicing. I'm practicing through my mistakes as I refuse to allow fear to overtake me on this journey.

April J. Lisbon

You have everything you need within you to be a great person and a great mother of a child with ASD. Even when the struggles come, and the physical and verbal rants ensue, just know that you have everything you need within you to support your child with ASD. It is the love you give and your commitment to walk this journey that makes you a powerful mom.

I applaud you, my fellow ASD moms. We were built for this lifestyle!

References

Altomare, A. A., McCrimmon, A. W., Cappadocia, M. C., Weiss, J. A., Beran, T. N., & Smith-

American Psychiatric Association. (2000). *Diagnostic and statistical manual of mental disorders*, (4th ed., text revision). Washington, DC: American Psychiatric Association.

Anderson-Abram, V. (2018, January). *There is purpose in your pain.* Virtual Tele-Summit presented at the 1st quarter New beginnings: Self-discovery Speakers Tour.

Blumberg, S. J., Bramlett, M. D., Kogan, M. D., Schieve, L. A., Jones, J. R., & Lu, M. C. (2013). *Changes in prevalence of parent-reported Autism Spectrum Disorder in school-aged US children: 2007 to 2011-2012* (No. 65). US Department of Health and Human Services, Centers for Disease Control and Prevention, National Center for Health Statistics.

Demers, A. D. (2017). When push comes to shove: How are students with Autism Spectrum Disorder coping with bullying?. *Canadian Journal of School Psychology, 32*(3-4), 209-227.

Grossi, D., Marcone, R., Cinquegrana, T., & Gallucci, M. (2013). On the differential nature of induced and incidental echolalia in autism. *Journal of Intellectual Disability Research, 57*(10), 903-912.

Hayes, S. A., & Watson, S. L. (2013). The impact of parenting stress: A meta-analysis of studies comparing the experience of parenting stress in parents of children with and without Autism Spectrum Disorder. *Journal of Autism and Developmental Disorders, 43*(3), 629-642.

Lord, C., & Bishop, S. L. (2010). Autism Spectrum Disorders. *Social Policy Report, 24*(2), 1-26.

Somerville, L. H. (2013). The teenage brain: Sensitivity to social evaluation. *Current directions in psychological science, 22*(2), 121-127.

Tsaousis, I. (2016). The relationship of self-esteem to bullying perpetration and peer victimization among schoolchildren and adolescents: a meta-analytic review. *Aggression and Violent Behavior, 31*, 186-199.

www.ingramcontent.com/pod-product-compliance
Lightning Source LLC
Chambersburg PA
CBHW030455010526
44118CB00011B/944